ANIMAL SUPERSTARS

RHINOCEROS BEETLE

HEAVYWEIGHT CHAMPION

PAIGE V. POLINSKY

CONSULTING EDITOR, DIANE CRAIG, M.A./READING SPECIALIST

Super Sandcastle

An Imprint of Abdo Publishing
abdopublishing.com

abdopublishing.com

Published by Abdo Publishing, a division of ABDO, PO Box 398166, Minneapolis, Minnesota 55439. Copyright © 2017 by Abdo Consulting Group, Inc. International copyrights reserved in all countries. No part of this book may be reproduced in any form without written permission from the publisher. Super SandCastle™ is a trademark and logo of Abdo Publishing.

Printed in the United States of America, North Mankato, Minnesota
062016
092016

 THIS BOOK CONTAINS
RECYCLED MATERIALS

Editor: Rebecca Felix
Content Developer: Nancy Tuminelly, Mighty Media, Inc.
Cover and Interior Design and Production: Christa Schneider, Mighty Media, Inc.
Photo Credits: Mighty Media, Inc.; Shutterstock

Library of Congress Cataloging-in-Publication Data

Names: Polinsky, Paige V., author.
Title: Rhinoceros beetle : heavyweight champion / by Paige V. Polinsky.
Description: Minneapolis, Minnesota : Abdo Publishing, [2017] | Series:
   Animal superstars
Identifiers: LCCN 2016006321 (print) | LCCN 2016007329 (ebook) | ISBN
   9781680781502 (print) | ISBN 9781680775938 (ebook)
Subjects: LCSH: Rhinoceros beetle--Juvenile literature.
Classification: LCC QL596.S3 P65 2016 (print) | LCC QL596.S3 (ebook) | DDC
   595.76/49--dc23
LC record available at http://lccn.loc.gov/2016006321

Super SandCastle™ books are created by a team of professional educators, reading specialists, and content developers around five essential components— phonemic awareness, phonics, vocabulary, text comprehension, and fluency—to assist young readers as they develop reading skills and strategies and increase their general knowledge. All books are written, reviewed, and leveled for guided reading, early reading intervention, and Accelerated Reader™ programs for use in shared, guided, and independent reading and writing activities to support a balanced approach to literacy instruction.

CONTENTS

BIG BUGS 4

HUGE HORNS 6

SUPER STRENGTH 8

AWESOME ARMOR 10

LEAFY LIVING 12

SWEET TREATS 14

TAKING FLIGHT 16

BUG BABIES 18

PEOPLE PROBLEMS 20

RHINOCEROS BEETLE SUPERSTAR 22

WHAT DO YOU KNOW ABOUT RHINOCEROS BEETLES? 23

GLOSSARY 24

BIG BUGS

Rhinoceros beetles are insects. There are more than 300 **species** of this beetle. Most are very large. Some are 7 inches (18 cm) long!

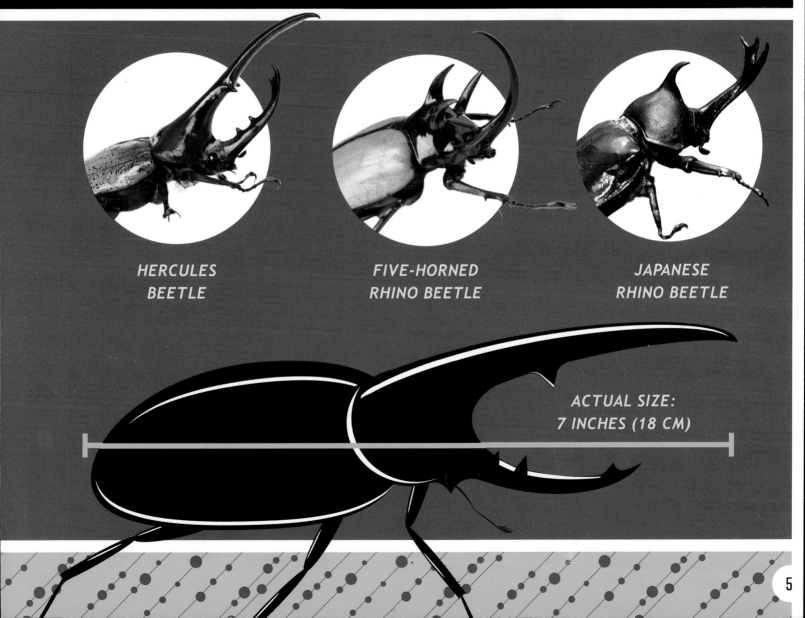

HERCULES
BEETLE

FIVE-HORNED
RHINO BEETLE

JAPANESE
RHINO BEETLE

ACTUAL SIZE:
7 INCHES (18 CM)

HUGE HORNS

Male rhino beetles have large horns. They use them to battle. They fight over females. Each **species** has a different fighting style.

SUPER STRENGTH

Some rhino beetles are very strong. The Hercules beetle is one. It can lift about 850 times its weight!

HOW MUCH?

THE HERCULES BEETLE LIFTING 850 TIMES ITS WEIGHT IS **AMAZING.**
IT WOULD BE LIKE A PERSON LIFTING NINE ELEPHANTS!

AWESOME ARMOR

Rhino beetles' shells protect them. Most are black or gray. They can also be shades of brown, or even green. Some shells also have soft hairs.

LEAFY LIVING

Rhino beetles live around the world. This includes every continent except Antarctica. The beetles live in dead leaves and logs.

NORTH
AMERICA

EUROPE

ASIA

AFRICA

SOUTH
AMERICA

AUSTRALIA

MAP KEY

● = WHERE RHINO
BEETLES LIVE

Rhino beetles are **nocturnal**. They search for food at night.

SWEET TREATS

Rhino beetles eat sugary foods.
These include fruit and nectar.
They also eat tree **sap**.

BABY FOOD

A YOUNG RHINO BEETLE'S DIET AFFECTS ITS **FUTURE** HORN SHAPE.

TAKING FLIGHT

Rhino beetles have wings. They are able to fly. But some people think they look **clumsy**.

WING SOUNDS

RHINO BEETLES SQUEAK AND HISS. THEY RUB THEIR WINGS AGAINST THEIR BODIES TO MAKE THESE SOUNDS.

BUG BABIES

Female rhino beetles mate once. They then lay about 50 eggs. The eggs hatch into larvae. The beetles become adults after **molting** many times.

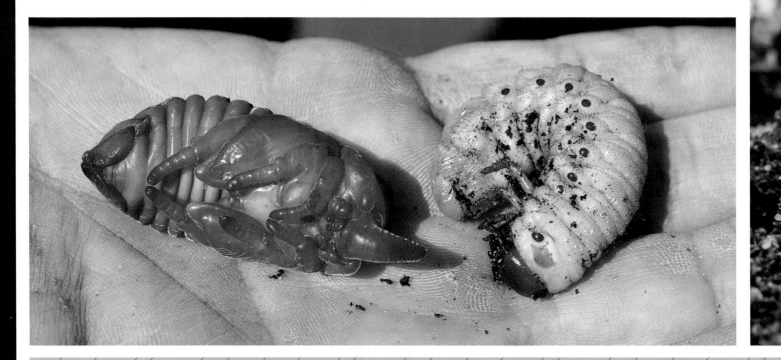

PEOPLE PROBLEMS

Rhino beetles are sold as pets in Asia. This is creating a problem. Wild rhino beetle populations are **shrinking**. Another problem is **deforestation**. It destroys the beetles' homes.

RHINO BEETLES FOR SALE IN ASIA

BEETLE BATTLES

WATCHING RHINO BEETLE FIGHTS IS A POPULAR **PASTIME** IN THAILAND.

RHINOCEROS BEETLE SUPERSTAR

Can you imagine a rhino beetle superstar? What **awards** would it win?

WHAT DO YOU KNOW ABOUT
RHINOCEROS BEETLES?

1. Most rhino beetles are very small.

True or false?

2. A shell protects rhino beetles from harm.

True or false?

3. Rhino beetles eat **sap**.

True or false?

4. Rhino beetles do not have wings.

True or false?

ANSWERS:
1. FALSE 2. TRUE 3. TRUE 4. FALSE

GLOSSARY

AMAZING - causing wonder or surprise.

AWARD - a prize.

CLUMSY - awkward and lacking grace.

DEFORESTATION - cutting down or burning all the trees in an area.

FUTURE - coming or happening at a later time.

MOLT - to shed feathers, fur, or another body covering.

NOCTURNAL - most active at night.

PASTIME - an enjoyable activity done in one's spare time.

SAP - liquid that is inside trees and plants.

SHRINK - to become smaller.

SPECIES - a group of animals or plants that are similar and can reproduce.